AGES 8-88

YES & KNOW ®* GAME BOOK

FASCINATING FACTS
&
FUN GAMES

HOURS AND HOURS OF "BY-YOURSELF ENJOYMENT"®*
FROM THE MAKERS OF YES & KNOW®* GAME BOOKS

LEE PUBLICATIONS
1100 W. BROADWAY, P.O. BOX 32120, LOUISVILLE, KENTUCKY 40232-2120

*Trademarks of STRY-LENKOFF CO, LLC.

AGES 8-88

YES & KNOW ®* GAME BOOK

Invisible Ink

FASCINATING FACTS
&
FUN GAMES

will give you hours and hours of fun and enjoyment.

However it is
IMPORTANT
to use the pen properly.

1. Pen should be used with very light pressure. Excessive pressure may damage the pen point, printing and paper.

2. Always replace the cap when not in use.

Pen may dry out, or not react properly, if the cap is left off too long. If this happens, immerse tip in clean water for a MAXIMUM of ONE MINUTE. Sometimes excessive or constant rubbing pressure may cause the end of the tip to glaze over, restricting the flow of ink. This can be corrected by punching a series of holes in the end of the tip with a pin.

For an extra **YKP WHITE** pen, mail $1.00 to cover postage and handling to:
LEE PUBLICATIONS
P.O Box 32120 • Louisville, KY 40232-2120
Be sure to specify **YKP WHITE** pen.

www.leemagicpen.com

ISBN 1-56297-001-1

TIC-TAC-TOE
Logic Game

How To Play:

1. In each game decide whether you will be **X** or **O**. Use your Yes & Know® pen to write your **X** or **O** on the line next to the game number. The other letter is your opponent's letter.

2. Then fill in the blank areas in the game grid, one at a time. Try to win, horizontally or vertically, before your opponent does. There are no diagonal wins in this Logic game.

3. There is logic to this game, so a good Tic-Tac-Toe player should almost never lose. Check(✓) the right line under each game to keep track of how many you win or lose.

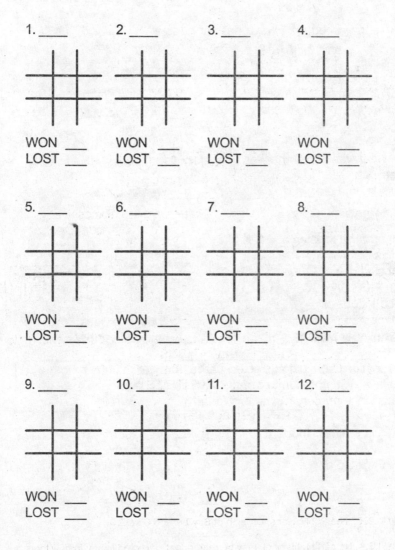

1. _____   2. _____   3. _____   4. _____

WON _____   WON _____   WON _____   WON _____
LOST _____ LOST _____ LOST _____ LOST _____

5. _____   6. _____   7. _____   8. _____

WON _____   WON _____   WON _____   WON _____
LOST _____ LOST _____ LOST _____ LOST _____

9. _____   10. _____   11. _____   12. _____

WON _____   WON _____   WON _____   WON _____
LOST _____ LOST _____ LOST _____ LOST _____

HOW MANY GAMES DID YOU WIN?   _____

NURSERY RHYME PEOPLE

Finish the nursery rhyme lines below by using your Yes & Know® pen to rub the space next to the answer you think is right. If NO appears, keep trying until you find YES. When you have finished, follow the directions on the bottom of the page.

1. Leave them alone, and they'll come home, wagging their
_____ tails behind them   _____ friends to play
_____ little lost mittens   _____ curds and whey

2. Could eat no fat, his wife could eat no
_____ meat   _____ lean
_____ veggies   _____ cream

3. Which was against the rules. It made the children
_____ sing and dance   _____ shoo him away
_____ run away   _____ laugh and play

4. Went to the cupboard, to give her poor dog a
_____ bone   _____ drink
_____ biscuit   _____ can of food

5. He caught fishes, in other men's
_____ lakes   _____ fishbowls
_____ ponds   _____ ditches

6. When she was good, she was very, very good, and when she was bad, she was
_____ put in time out   _____ terrible
_____ horrid   _____ very, very bad

7. Went up a hill to fetch a
_____ glass of milk   _____ pail of water
_____ bucket of ice   _____ bowl of porridge

8. Picked a peck of
_____ peppered pickles   _____ prickly pickles
_____ purple peppers   _____ pickled peppers

All the questions you just answered came from the nursery rhymes listed below. Write the number of the question on the line in front of the name of the nursery rhyme it is found in.

_____ A. Old Mother Hubbard   _____ E. Little Tommy Tittlemouse

_____ B. Jack Sprat   _____ F. The Little Girl with a Curl

_____ C. Jack and Jill   _____ G. Mary Had a Little Lamb

_____ D. Little Bo Peep   _____ H. Peter Piper

Fill in the answer box to see how many you got right.

WHAT DOES MOLLY LIKE?

Molly likes posters, but not signs.

Molly likes stripes, but not lines.

Molly likes blasts, but not explosions.

Molly likes history, but not dates.

Molly likes dust, but not dirt.

Molly likes pastures, but not fields.

Molly likes festivals, but not parties.

Molly likes investments, but not money.

Molly likes streams, but not rivers.

Molly likes streets, but not roads.

DO YOU KNOW WHAT MOLLY LIKES?

Write your answer on this line. _____

Fill in the box to see if you are right.

Molly likes pennies, but not dimes.

Molly likes movies, but not television.

Molly likes cookies, but not cake.

Molly likes horses, but not dogs.

Molly likes baseball, but not golf.

Molly likes summer, but not fall.

Molly likes scooters, but not bicycles.

Molly likes inches, but not feet.

Molly likes winter, but not spring.

Molly likes sweaters, but not coats.

DO YOU KNOW WHAT MOLLY LIKES?

Write your answer on this line. _____

Fill in the box to see if you are right.

BINGO
DIRECTIONS

OBJECT:
1. To "cover" any five numbers on the **BINGO** card that are in line—vertically, horizontally, or diagonally. One of the spaces may be the center FREE SPACE.
or
2. To "cover" all four corners of the card.
You **WIN** if you do either of the above before your "imaginary opponent" does.

HOW TO PLAY:
Select any block in the chart above a **BINGO** card. Fill it in with your Yes & Know® pen. If a number appears, and that number is on your **BINGO** card, fill in its box until a dot appears (that number is "covered").
Keep playing until you **WIN** or a "B" appears instead of a number. If "B" appears, your opponent has called **"BINGO,"** and you **LOSE**.

B (1-15)	I (16-30)	N (31-45)	G (46-60)	O (61-75)	B (1-15)	I (16-30)	N (31-45)	G (46-60)	O (61-75)
7	25	41	48	72	9	30	42	56	64
14	21	33	57	66	15	24	36	47	73
3	18	FREE SPACE	60	75	6	19	FREE SPACE	58	75
8	16	40	52	61	5	22	39	60	71
10	27	43	49	68	2	29	32	51	62

DO YOU REMEMBER?

Leader of the Dwarfs
_____ Sleepy   _____ Grumpy
_____ Doc   _____ Happy

Sang "When You Wish Upon a Star"
_____ Geppetto   _____ Pinocchio
_____ The Blue Fairy   _____ Jiminy Cricket

Dumbo's little friend
_____ Randy Rabbit   _____ Timothy Mouse
_____ Pierre Poodle   _____ Tony Weasel

Bambi's rabbit friend
_____ Fluffy   _____ Peter
_____ Thumper   _____ Puff

Geppetto's pet cat
_____ Gideon   _____ Figaro
_____ Foulfellow   _____ Stromboli

Sang "I'm Late"
_____ White Rabbit   _____ Alice
_____ Mad Hatter   _____ March Hare

Nurse-dog in <u>Peter Pan</u>
_____ Tiger Lily   _____ Darling
_____ Tinker   _____ Nana

Told the Queen Snow White was still alive
_____ the Dwarfs   _____ the Huntsman
_____ Prince Charming   _____ Magic Mirror

Whale that swallowed Pinocchio
_____ Monstro   _____ Lampwick
_____ Moby   _____ Worthy

Bambi's lady love
_____ Sandi   _____ Faline
_____ Dawn   _____ Sunny

Grew longer and longer when Pinocchio lied
_____ his arms   _____ his legs
_____ his nose   _____ his hair

The Queen tried to kill Snow White with a
_____ magic spell   _____ poisoned apple
_____ poisoned drink   _____ hunting knife

Bambi's friend Flower was a
_____ rose   _____ robin
_____ doe   _____ skunk

BULL'S-EYE
DIRECTIONS

Your teacher has given you a list of art supplies to try to find before next week's class. The object is to find the supplies listed below by uncovering the letters in their names before your time runs out.

Fill in any one of the 52 spaces in the bull's-eye with your Yes & Know® pen. If a letter appears, fill in a circle under that letter in one of the supplies below. If a star appears, fill in its circle in the time box.

You have found an item on the list when you have uncovered all of the letters in its name. If you uncover all four stars, your time has run out and you are ready to go back to art class. Don't worry if you didn't find all of the supplies, your teacher has some extras.

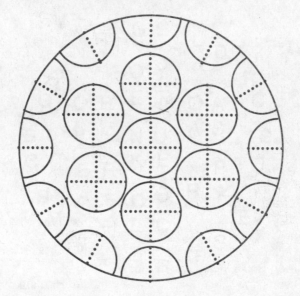

1. S C I S S O R S
   O O O O O O O O

2. M A R K E R S
   O O O O O O

3. C R A Y O N S
   O O O O O O O

4. G L I T T E R
   O O O O O O O

5. C O L O R E D   P A P E R
   O O O O O O O O O O O

6. G L U E
   O O O O

7. P E N
   O O O

TIME BOX

How many supplies did you find?

MATCHING—MOVIE ANIMALS

All the animals below were in Disney movies. Match each of the animals (A-L) to its name/ names in the list (1-12) below. With your Yes & Know® pen, write the letter of the animal on the line in front of the name/names it was called in the movie.

A. Monkey	D. Mandrill	G. Parrot	J. Crab
B. Meerkat	E. Mice	H. Hornbill	K. Hyenas
C. Dog	F. Warthog	I. Fish	L. Cats

____ 1. Pumbaa

____ 2. Zazu

____ 3. Rafiki

____ 4. Bruno

____ 5. Sebastian

____ 6. Abu

____ 7. Gus and Jaq

____ 8. Timon

____ 9. Iago

____ 10. Si and Am

____ 11. Flounder

____ 12. Shenzi, Banzai, and Ed

Fill in the answer box to see how many you got right.

All the animals above were in the movies listed below. Write the numbers of the animals on the line next to the movie they appeared in.

A. Cinderella _____

B. The Little Mermaid _____

C. The Lion King _____

D. Aladdin _____

E. Lady and the Tramp _____

Fill in the answer box to see how many you got right.

BASEBALL
DIRECTIONS

YOUR TEAM IS UP TO BAT. IT IS THE BOTTOM OF THE NINTH INNING. THE OPPOSING TEAM IS AHEAD 1 TO 0.

GAME RULES

1. If your team can get four hits (including walks) you will score two runs and WIN, since base runners sometimes advance more than one base.
2. If you get three hits (including walks) you will score one run. The game will be TIED but the extra innings will not be played.
3. If you score less than three hits (including walks) YOU LOSE.

HOW TO PLAY

1. With your pen fill in any one of the small boxes in the PITCHED BALL CHART. It will show "B" for ball, "S" for strike, "O" for out, or "H" for hit. Record the ball, strike, out, or hit by filling in the correct box in the SCORE CHART under BALLS, STRIKES, OUTS, or HITS for Batter #1.
2. Continue until Batter #1:
   a. Has three strikes or an out—you fill in the box under OUT, or
   b. Has four balls—you fill in the box under HITS or WALKS, or
   c. Gets a hit—you fill in the box under HITS or WALKS.
3. Then go on to Batter #2, etc.
4. Continue until your team has three OUTS or four HITS or WALKS.

PITCHED BALL CHART

4 HITS or WALKS – YOU WIN
3 HITS or WALKS – YOU TIE
LESS THAN 3 HITS or WALKS – YOU LOSE

SCORE CHART

BATTER	BALLS				STRIKES			OUTS	HITS or WALKS
BATTER #1									
BATTER #2									
BATTER #3									
BATTER #4									
BATTER #5									
BATTER #6									

TOTAL – Use your Yes & Know® pen to write in your score.

IN A WORD OR TWO OR THREE OR FOUR

The Great Bear constellation
_____ Ursa Minor   _____ Cygnus
_____ Taurus   _____ Ursa Major

Often called America's national pastime
_____ football   _____ baseball
_____ basketball   _____ soccer

"Astronaut" means
_____ airplane pilot   _____ sailor among the stars
_____ brave person   _____ space explorer

A game that uses love and advantage in its scoring system
_____ cricket   _____ rugby
_____ volleyball   _____ tennis

Liquid part of blood
_____ red blood cells   _____ white blood cells
_____ platelets   _____ plasma

First day of Lent
_____ Black Friday   _____ Ash Wednesday
_____ Palm Sunday   _____ Blue Monday

"The land down under"
_____ Africa   _____ New Zealand
_____ Australia   _____ South America

European country shaped like a boot
_____ Norway   _____ Italy
_____ Ireland   _____ Spain

Color of belt worn by karate experts
_____ black   _____ green
_____ white   _____ brown

Number of letters in the Hawaiian alphabet
_____ 26   _____ 12
_____ 20   _____ 31

The Bering Strait separates Alaska from
_____ the lower 48 states   _____ Canada
_____ Russia   _____ Ireland

In a computer, number of bits in a byte
_____ 10   _____ 2
_____ 100   _____ 8

Takedown and full nelson are terms in
_____ hockey   _____ football
_____ wrestling   _____ chess

OPPOSITES

Use your Yes & Know® pen to write the opposite of the words below on the answer lines next to each word. When you have filled in all the words, the first letter of the words, reading down, will tell you the favorite subject of a lot of schoolchildren. Then fill in the spaces inside the answer boxes to see how many you got right.

ANSWERS

PULL   ___ ___ ___ ___

SAD   ___ ___ ___ ___ ___

OLD   ___ ___ ___ ___

FAST   ___ ___ ___ ___

OUTSIDE   ___ ___ ___ ___ ___ ___

DIRTY   ___ ___ ___ ___ ___

UNCLE   ___ ___ ___ ___

HIGH   ___ ___ ___

EXIT   ___ ___ ___ ___ ___

WET   ___ ___ ___

DOWNHILL   ___ ___ ___ ___ ___ ___

THROW   ___ ___ ___ ___

PRESENT   ___ ___ ___ ___ ___ ___

LISTEN   ___ ___ ___ ___

OUT OF   ___ ___ ___ ___

UNDER   ___ ___ ___ ___

SOUTH   ___ ___ ___ ___ ___

UGLY   ___ ___ ___ ___ ___ ___

FRIEND   ___ ___ ___ ___ ___

FIND THE TWINS

The characters below may all look alike, but only two are really twins. With your Yes & Know® pen fill in the boxes under the two you think are identical. The boxes under the true twins will tell you their names. Keep trying until you find them.

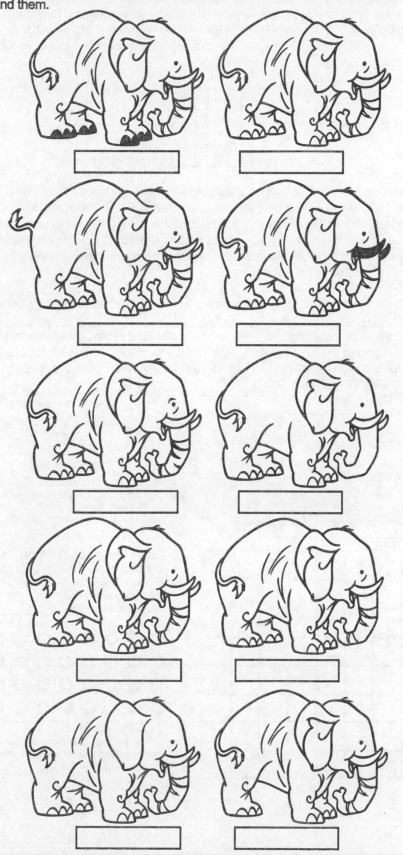

FLEET
DIRECTIONS

OBJECT:
To completely destroy all ships in the enemy fleet in the 32 shots you are allowed. The fleet consists of a **BATTLESHIP** represented by five **B**'s, a **CRUISER**—four **C**'s, a **DESTROYER**—three **D**'s, and a **SUBMARINE**-two **S**'s. Boxes where ships are located are always next to each other in horizontal, vertical, or diagonal lines.

EXAMPLE

B						S	S
B						D	
B					D		
B				D			
B							
	C	C	C	C			

HOW TO PLAY:

1. Attempt to make a hit on an invisible ship by choosing a box in the grid and filling it in. If an **X** appears, you MISSED. If one of the other letters appear, you have made a hit and the letter tells you the type of ship. You must hit every box of the ship to destroy it. Each time you shoot (fill in a box in the grid), you must check off the shot in one of the 32 circles in the Shot Record.

2. To WIN you must destroy all four enemy ships before you run out of shots.

Two can play by using two fleets at the same time. Each player takes a turn shooting at his opponent's fleet. When two play there is no limit to the number of shots; the first one to completely destroy his opponent's fleet wins the game.

Each Fleet consists of:
Battleship--BBBBB
Cruiser--CCCC
Destroyer--DDD
Submarine--SS

O O O O O O O O
O O O O O O O O
O O O O O O O O
O O O O O O O O

32 Shot Record
Fill in one of the above circles each time you shoot at the Fleet at the left.

MAIN STREET

This is Main Street in Newton, U.S.A.
Can you guess the name of each store in the picture?

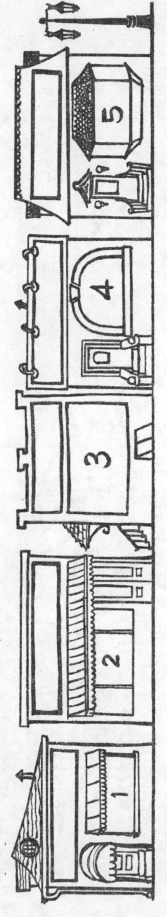

READ THESE CLUES

1. You can buy something to eat at stores 1, 3, and 5. The ice-cream store is between two stores.

2. After buying a book, you pass the ice-cream store on the way to get a hair cut. The book store is nearer to the street light than is the barbershop.

3. If you tried to buy a ham in the store next to the street light, the clerk would tell you to go to the last store on the block.

4. One of the stores is a bakery.

With the above clues you should know the name of each store in the picture.

By each name below, fill in with your Yes & Know® pen the store number that you consider correct.

Ice-Cream Shop	Barbershop
1 __ 2 __ 3 __ 4 __ 5 __	1 __ 2 __ 3 __ 4 __ 5 __

Bookstore	Butcher
1 __ 2 __ 3 __ 4 __ 5 __	1 __ 2 __ 3 __ 4 __ 5 __

Bakery

1 __ 2 __ 3 __ 4 __ 5 __

When you finish, color in the signs on the pictures above and watch the correct names of the stores pop up!

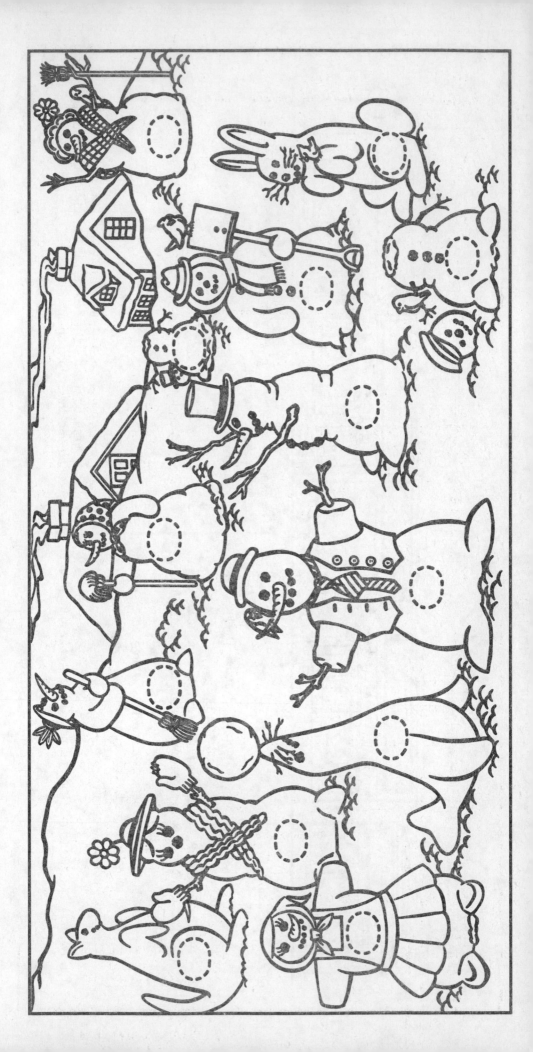

LINE UP . . . SNOW SCULPTURE CONTEST . . . LINE UP

The first snowstorm has come to your city. Your neighborhood is having a snow sculpture contest for the children in an empty lot on the corner of your street. Yesterday, on your way home from school, you set your backpack down in the lot to play. You went home without it and, now, one of the sculptures is sitting on it. You will have to use the clues to the right to find your backpack without destroying all of the sculptures.

Choose any clue and fill in its answer space with your Yes & Know® pen. After each clue, try to find your backpack by choosing a snow sculpture and filling in the dotted area on the sculpture you think is sitting on your backpack. If NO appears, try another clue. If you find the backpack in one or two tries you have time to rebuild the sculptures and no one knows the difference. If it takes you three or four, some of your friends are pretty mad that you tore down their sculptures. They think you did it because their sculptures were better than yours, and you wanted to win the contest. If it takes five or more, your homework doesn't get done and you are in big trouble at school, and at home because you have ruined the contest.

CLUES

Is the snow sculpture an animal?

Is it holding an object?

Is there a bird on it?

Has its head been knocked off?

Does it have coal buttons?

Does it have branches for arms?

Does it have a carrot nose?

Does it have a hat?

ANSWERS

HANGMAN
DIRECTIONS

OBJECT:
To figure out the secret word represented by the numbered blank spaces before being hanged.

HOW TO PLAY:

1. Every letter in the alphabet is printed below the HANGMAN. Choose any letter and with your Yes & Know® pen, fill in the box under it. If the letter you choose is in the secret word, a number (or numbers) will appear in the box. With your pen, print that letter on that numbered line (or lines) next to the HANGMAN. After several letters are found, the word will begin to take shape.
2. If the letter you choose is not in the word, NO will appear. For each NO you must fill in one of the 16 parts of the HANGMAN. The parts are: 2 ears, 2 eyes, nose, mouth, face (remainder of head), body, 2 arms, 2 hands, 2 legs, and 2 feet.
3. If all 16 parts of the man are filled in before you complete the word, you lose. If you complete the word first, you win!

__ O O D __ L __ C K

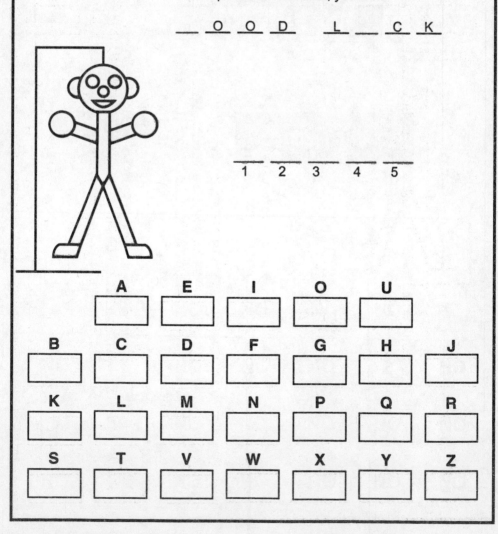

__ __ __ __ __
1 2 3 4 5

A   E   I   O   U

B   C   D   F   G   H   J

K   L   M   N   P   Q   R

S   T   V   W   X   Y   Z

HANGMAN

A PLAY ON WORDS

Look at each picture below and spell out its name. Then mark the word that can be made by rearranging all the letters of the word you have spelled.

	___ least	___ clasp	___ cleats	___ stack
	___ rock	___ crack	___ corn	___ rack
	___ pealed	___ plain	___ pains	___ panel
	___ short	___ heard	___ roses	___ shore
	___ lost	___ loots	___ sooty	___ slows
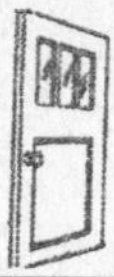	___ odor	___ drool	___ deal	___ dart
	___ vetoes	___ stave	___ save	___ votes
	___ traps	___ seat	___ rats	___ stare
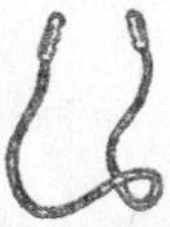	___ pros	___ pore	___ poor	___ prove
	___ low	___ wool	___ awl	___ law
	___ sieve	___ vast	___ save	___ stave
	___ bulb	___ balm	___ bum	___ bomb

TEST YOUR MEMORY

Study the picture carefully. Then turn to the next page to see how many questions you can answer correctly.

TEST YOUR MEMORY

How much do you remember about the picture? No fair looking back.

What kind of room is in the picture?
_____ bedroom   _____ kitchen
_____ classroom   _____ living room

How many children are in the picture?
_____ six   _____ ten
_____ nine   _____ eleven

What is NOT on the teachers desk?
_____ apple   _____ banana
_____ bell   _____ pencil

How many windows are in the room?
_____ one   _____ three
_____ two   _____ four

How many letters of the alphabet are on the wall?
_____ three   _____ ten
_____ five   _____ eleven

What kind of book is the girl sitting in front reading?
_____ history   _____ English
_____ poems   _____ geography

Which of these letters is written on the wall?
_____ A   _____ F
_____ W   _____ T

What is the teacher doing?
_____ reading   _____ pointing
_____ sitting   _____ dancing

How many children have ribbons in their hair?
_____ two   _____ five
_____ three   _____ seven

Where is the stove in the room?
_____ in the front   _____ on the right side
_____ in the back   _____ on the left side

What rule is posted on the wall?
_____ bronze   _____ silver
_____ golden   _____ blue

What animal is looking in the window?
_____ a cat   _____ a dog
_____ a squirrel   _____ a rabbit

TIC-TAC-TOE
Luck Game

Game Rules:
1. In this game you are always **X**.
2. Every game contains an invisible **X** winning arrangement.

How To Play:
1. With your Yes & Know® pen fill in the blank areas in the game grid, one at a time, until you find the horizontal, vertical, or diagonal X arrangement.

2. If you can do it in 5 tries or less, you are LUCKY; 6 tries AVERAGE; 7 or more UNLUCKY.

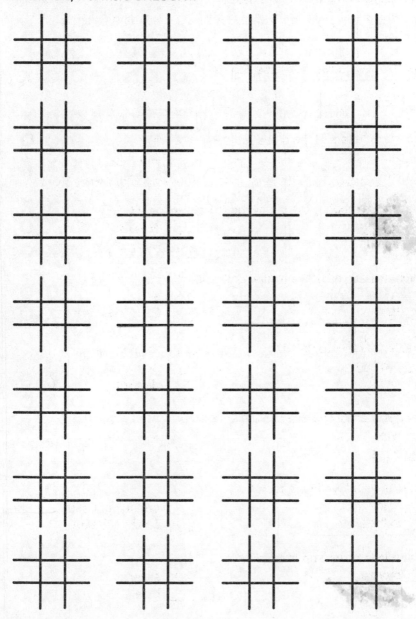

HOW MANY GAMES WERE YOU LUCKY?   _____

AVERAGE?   _____

UNLUCKY?   _____

RIDDLES

Fill in the balloom shapes with your Yes & Know® pen to find the answers.

What is purple and black, has long orange claws, weighs 7,000 pounds, can fly through the air at a speed of 600 miles per hour, and sings lullabies to the birds at midnight when it snows?

$\big(\qquad\qquad\big)$

What were the first words Paul Revere said when he finished his famous ride?

$\big(\qquad\qquad\big)$

What does a little-bitty white baby lamb become after it's seven days old?

$\big(\qquad\qquad\big)$

My name is spelled with three letters, but if you take two of my letters away, I still have the same name. what am I?

(TEA)

What fruit do you always study in your history lessons at school?

$\big(\qquad\qquad\big)$

What word becomes shorter when you add a syllable to it?

$\big(\qquad\qquad\big)$

If the entire city of Chicago, Illinois, would sink, what would float?

$\big(\qquad\qquad\big)$

Do you know the name of a room that boys and girls can eat?

$\big(\qquad\qquad\big)$

What word is always pronounced wrong?

(WRONG)

Why does the Statue of Liberty stand on Liberty Island?

$\big(\qquad\qquad\qquad\big)$

WHAT DOES MOLLY LIKE?

Molly likes bread, but not butter.

Molly likes barns, but not cows.

Molly likes candy, but not chocolate.

Molly likes girls, but not ladies.

Molly likes coats, but not sweaters.

Molly likes salad, but not lettuce.

Molly likes jelly, but not jam.

Molly likes black, but not gray.

Molly likes books, but not magazines.

Molly likes March, but not September.

DO YOU KNOW WHAT MOLLY LIKES?

Write your answer on this line. _____

Fill in the box to see if you are right.

SHE LIKES FIVE-LETTER WORDS.

Molly likes Eddie, but not Chad.

Molly likes Andrew, but not Billy.

Molly likes Elizabeth, but not Cathy.

Molly likes Oscar, but not Felix.

Molly likes Eric, but not Matthew.

Molly likes Irene, but not Rebecca.

Molly likes Emily, but not Lauren.

Molly likes Abigale, but not Sara.

Molly likes Ivan, but not Nolan.

Molly likes Allison, but not Taylor.

DO YOU KNOW WHAT MOLLY LIKES?

Write your answer on this line. _____

Fill in the box to see if you are right.

AMES STARTING WITH VOWELS.

BINGO

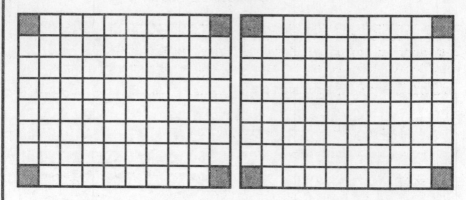

B (1-15)	I (16-30)	N (31-45)	G (46-60)	O (61-75)
5	23	34	47	68
13	18	35	59	61
2	16	FREE SPACE	49	70
7	29	41	53	65
10	22	31	50	72

B (1-15)	I (16-30)	N (31-45)	G (46-60)	O (61-75)
11	19	40	52	64
3	27	32	55	66
1	22	FREE SPACE	48	73
6	20	37	60	75
4	30	45	53	74

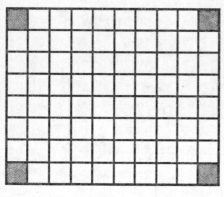
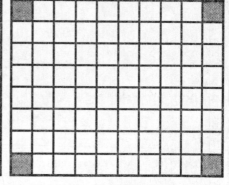

B (1-15)	I (16-30)	N (31-45)	G (46-60)	O (61-75)
3	24	39	58	67
9	18	43	60	69
15	30	FREE SPACE	48	75
10	19	44	57	71
4	25	38	51	62

B (1-15)	I (16-30)	N (31-45)	G (46-60)	O (61-75)
1	26	33	54	66
14	16	42	56	65
8	28	FREE SPACE	49	61
11	27	32	46	63
12	21	41	50	72

MATCHING—ANIMAL FACTS

Use your Yes & Know® pen to match each animal with the fact that best describes that animal. Write the letter of the fact on the line to the left of the animal's name. When you are finished, fill in the answer box to see how many you got right.

____ 1. Giraffe

____ 2. Bat

____ 3. Giant tortoise

____ 4. Cheetah

____ 5. Blue Whale

____ 6. Sailfish

____ 7. Chameleon

____ 8. Elephant

____ 9. Whale shark

____ 10. Giant squid

A. Largest of all animals

B. Largest fish

C. Largest eyes of all animals
   (the size of basketballs)

D. Tallest of all animals

E. Has a tongue as long as its body
   and can change the color of it's skin

F. Largest land animal

G. Fastest animal on land

H. Only mammal that can fly

I. Fastest animal in the water

J. Longest life span of all animals
   (can live more than 100 years)

ANSWER BOX:

Fill in the box below to learn more about animals.

BULL'S-EYE
DIRECTIONS

You are going to a ballgame with some of your friends. You have ten dollars to spend at the concession stand. The object is to see how much you can buy, by uncovering the letters in the names of the treats before your time runs out.

Fill in any one of the 52 spaces in the bull's-eye with your Yes & Know® pen. If a letter appears, fill in a circle under that letter in one of the treats below. If a star appears, fill in its circle in the time box.

You have bought a treat when you have uncovered all the letters in its name. If you uncover all four stars, your time has run out. The game is over and it is time to go home. When you have finished, fill in the boxes to the right of the treats you bought to see how much money you spent. How much money are you taking home?

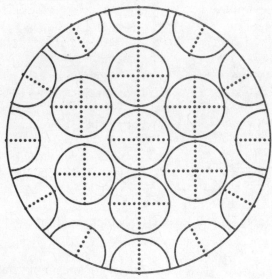

1. P O P C O R N
   O O O O O O O   ☐

2. C O R N   D O G
   O O O O   O O O   ☐

3. C A N D Y
   O O O O O   ☐

4. P E A N U T S
   O O O O O O O   ☐

5. S O D A
   O O O O   ☐

6. B I G   P R E T Z E L
   O O O   O O O O O O O   ☐

7. S N O W   C O N E
   O O O O   O O O O   ☐

TIME BOX
☆☆☆☆
O O O O

BASKETBALL
DIRECTIONS

You are the HOME TEAM in the finals of the championship basketball tournament. The score is tied at the end of the game. In this game, the first team to score 10 points or more in the overtime period will win the game.

HOW TO PLAY:
1. You must shoot for yourself, the HOME TEAM, and then for the VISITING TEAM. Choose any shot on the HOME TEAM side of the court and fill it in with your Yes & Know® pen to reveal the results. Then shoot for the VISITING TEAM on their side of the court.
2. Continue alternating shots until one team scores 10 points. The possible shots are:
    - 2 = 2 points
    - ★ = 2 points and the ball stolen for another shot - shoot again
    - F = Foul - choose and fill in any shot on the FREE THROW CHART
    - W = Walked - that team loses the ball - other team shoots
    - O = Missed shot - no points, other team shoots
    - S = Ball stolen by opponent - other team's turn
3. Keep score on the SCORE BOARD by filling in the blocks as you score points. Keep score for the VISITING TEAM also.

NOTE: Two people can play this game. One being the HOME TEAM, the other the VISITING TEAM.

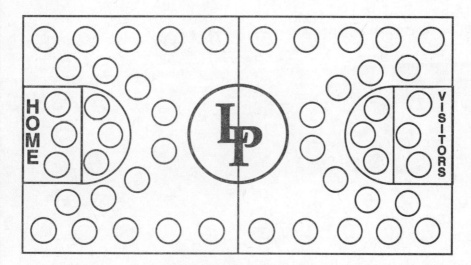

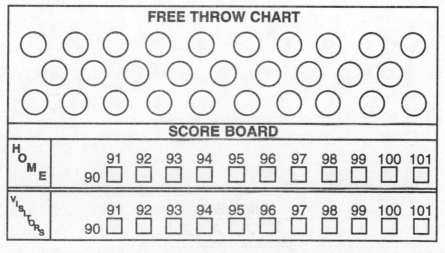

FREE THROW CHART

SCORE BOARD

HOME	90	91	92	93	94	95	96	97	98	99	100	101
□		□	□	□	□	□	□	□	□	□	□	□

VISITORS	90	91	92	93	94	95	96	97	98	99	100	101
□		□	□	□	□	□	□	□	□	□	□	□

"SNOITINIFED"

The quiz below may look easy, but there's a trick. All the answers have been spelled backwards. Can you find them? Doog kcul!

An old superstition says frogs cause

_____ snip   _____ sag   _____ bats   _____ straw

In fairy tales, an ugly giant is called an

_____ edit   _____ eros   _____ ergo   _____ ban

A hammer is a very useful

_____ loot   _____ tug   _____ par   _____ nub

Another word for "boast" is

_____ gut   _____ gab   _____ garb   _____ gas

Something to sit on is a

_____ spools   _____ sloops   _____ bun   _____ loots

Another name for a poet is a

_____ dam   _____ drab   _____ ram   _____ dab

Movie film is wound around a

_____ raw   _____ pin   _____ leer   _____ bus

A shoulder purse has a long

_____ parts   _____ don   _____ won   _____ wen

Water on the grass at early morning is called

_____ was   _____ wed   _____ lap   _____ mid

Someone's clothes could also be called their

_____ bat   _____ bad   _____ tip   _____ brag

A girl's nickname might be

_____ gem   _____ bag   _____ dim   _____ mar

A type of sailing ship is a

_____ spool   _____ straw   _____ loops   _____ pools

BASEBALL

PITCHED BALL CHART

4 HITS or WALKS – YOU WIN
3 HITS or WALKS – YOU TIE
LESS THAN 3 HITS or WALKS – YOU LOSE

SCORE CHART

BATTER	BALLS				STRIKES			OUTS	HITS or WALKS
BATTER #1									
BATTER #2									
BATTER #3									
BATTER #4									
BATTER #5									
BATTER #6									

TOTAL – Use your Yes & Know® pen to write in your score.

PITCHED BALL CHART

4 HITS or WALKS – YOU WIN
3 HITS or WALKS – YOU TIE
LESS THAN 3 HITS or WALKS – YOU LOSE

SCORE CHART

BATTER	BALLS				STRIKES			OUTS	HITS or WALKS
BATTER #1									
BATTER #2									
BATTER #3									
BATTER #4									
BATTER #5									
BATTER #6									

TOTAL – Use your Yes & Know® pen to write in your score.

NAME THIS PLACE

Use your Yes & Know® pen to answer the questions below. If your answer is right, a letter will appear; if your answer is wrong, a NO will appear. Keep trying until you find the right answer.

When you have finished all of the questions, write the correct answer letter on the line/lines on the bottom of the page that have the same number as the question the letter appeared in. When you have filled in the lines you will see the name of the invisible picture that is in the box on the next page. Fill in the box with your pen to see the picture.

1. American football is played by two teams of

   ___   ___   ___   ___
    5   7   9   11

2. Canadian football is played by two teams of

   ___   ___   ___   ___
   10   11   12   13

3. Soccer is played by two teams of

   ___   ___   ___   ___
    9   11   12   15

4. Basketball is played by two teams of

   ___   ___   ___   ___
    5   6   7   8

5. National League baseball is played by two teams of

   ___   ___   ___   ___
    8   9   10   11

6. American League baseball is almost always played by two teams of

   ___   ___   ___   ___
    8   9   10   11

7. Indoor volleyball is played by two teams of

   ___   ___   ___   ___
    2   3   4   6

8. Ice hockey is played by two teams of

   ___   ___   ___   ___
    5   6   8   9

9. Field hockey is played by two teams of

   ___   ___   ___   ___
    9   10   11   12

 ___ .   ___ .   ___   ___   ___   ___   ___   ___   ___
  8   4   9   2   5   6   1   7   3

Gently rub the spaces above the blank lines below to learn about this building.

The _____ _____ _____ is the building where _____ meets. It is located on _____ _____ in Washington, D.C.

The _____ has _____ rooms on _____ floors. The _____ wing is on the _____ side of the building. The _____ of _____ wing is on the _____ side of the building.

The center of the building has a huge _____ . On top of the _____ stands the _____ of _____ . Under the _____ is the grand _____ with paintings and sculptures of _____ and _____ in the nation's _____ . Also on this floor are two other _____ visitor areas; the _____ _____ _____ , which houses statues donated by the _____ of famous _____ , and the _____ _____ _____ .

FIND THE TWINS

The characters below may all look alike, but only two are really twins. With your Yes & Know® pen fill in the boxes under the two you think are identical. The boxes under the true twins will tell you their names. Keep trying until you find them.

FLEET

Each Fleet consists of:
Battleship--BBBBB
Cruiser--CCCC
Destroyer--DDD
Submarine--SS

O O O O O O O
O O O O O O O
O O O O O O O
O O O O O O O

32 Shot Record
Fill in one of the above
circles each time you shoot
at the Fleet at the left.

Each Fleet consists of:
Battleship--BBBBB
Cruiser--CCCC
Destroyer--DDD
Submarine--SS

O O O O O O O
O O O O O O O
O O O O O O O
O O O O O O O

32 Shot Record
Fill in one of the above
circles each time you shoot
at the Fleet at the left.

Each Fleet consists of:
Battleship--BBBBB
Cruiser--CCCC
Destroyer--DDD
Submarine--SS

O O O O O O O
O O O O O O O
O O O O O O O
O O O O O O O

32 Shot Record
Fill in one of the above
circles each time you shoot
at the Fleet at the left.

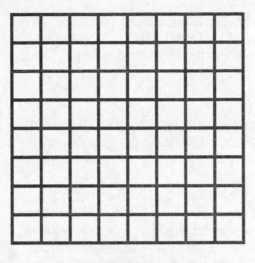
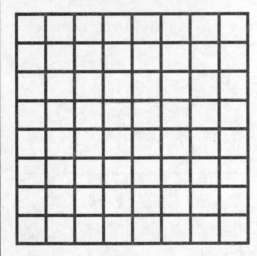
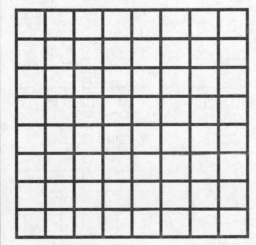

FOOTBALL
DIRECTIONS

YOU ARE THE QUARTERBACK IN THE BOWL GAME. YOUR TEAM IS BEHIND BY 3 POINTS WITH ONE MINUTE TO GO. YOU HAVE THE BALL ON YOUR OWN 20 YARD LINE AND IT IS YOUR JOB TO SCORE A TOUCHDOWN.

HOW TO PLAY:

1. Choose either a running or a passing play by filling in any box in the 1st Down row. If a number appears, move your ball on the field that number of yards by filling in the ball markers on the field. If 0 appears, there is no gain and you lose that down.
2. If you did not gain 10 yards on the 1st Down, fill in a box in the 2nd Down row. If you still haven't gone 10 yards, go to the 3rd Down row and choose a box. Anytime you have gone 10 yards or more you have won a 1st Down. Go back to the 1st Down row and start over.
3. If you didn't move 10 yards in 4 plays (downs), you lose. If an F (fumble) or I (interception) appears, you lose. If a T appears, you score a touchdown and your team wins the game.

NOTE: Running plays are safer. Passing plays give you more chance of a long gain, but also more chance of a 0.

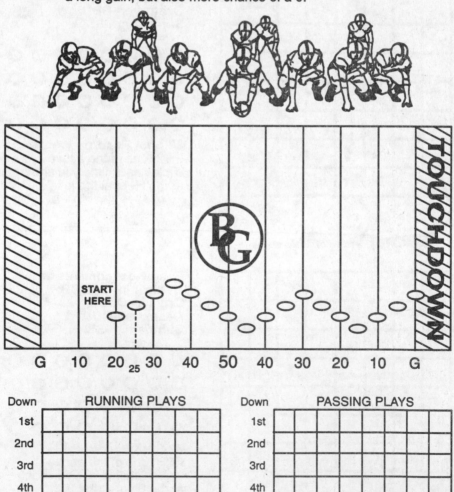

Down	RUNNING PLAYS						Down	PASSING PLAYS					
1st							1st						
2nd							2nd						
3rd							3rd						
4th							4th						

A BEAUTY OF A MOVIE

Sleeping Beauty's name
____ Princess Anna   ____ Princess Aurora
____ Princess Rose   ____ Princess Lavinia

Bad witch who cast an evil spell on Sleeping Beauty
____ Maleficent   ____ Gisele
____ Imelda   ____ Gwendolyn

Father of Sleeping Beauty
____ King Jonathan   ____ King Edward
____ King Henry   ____ King Stefan

Beauty's handsome Prince
____ Prince Charming   ____ Prince Matthew
____ Prince Phillip   ____ Prince Vincent

The Prince's father
____ King John   ____ King Andrew
____ King Lance   ____ King Hubert

The Prince's horse
____ Samson   ____ Duke
____ Shag   ____ Perry

Not one of the good fairies who raised Sleeping Beauty
____ Flora   ____ Flava
____ Fauna   ____ Merryweather

Sleeping Beauty slept for a total of
____ 100 years   ____ 50 years
____ 1000 years   ____ 10 years

Sleeping Beauty's' name when she lived with the fairies
____ Rose Red   ____ Rose White
____ Rosebud   ____ Briar Rose

The spell took effect when Beauty turned
____ thirteen   ____ twenty
____ sixteen   ____ twenty-one

The bad fairy had a pet
____ snake   ____ raven
____ dinosaur   ____ dragon

While fighting the Prince the bad fairy turned into a
____ dinosaur   ____ dragon
____ raging raven   ____ octopus

Evil protectors of the bad fairy
____ roras   ____ flocks
____ goons   ____ jesters

CLAIM TO FAME

Each person listed below has some claim to fame. Read each name and then look at the chart on top of the page. With your Yes & Know® pen fill in the space above the line next to the number you think is that person's claim to fame. If NO appears, try again. Some of the numbers will be used more than once.

1. U. S. President	4. Baseball Hitter	7. Inventor
2. American Idol Winner	5. Cyclist	8. Explorer
3. Olympic Ice Skater	6. Writer	9. Pro Golfer

Tiger Woods   1 ____   4 ____   5 ____   9 ____

George Bush   1 ____   5 ____   6 ____   8 ____

Dr. Seuss   5 ____   6 ____   7 ____   8 ____

Alexander Graham Bell 1 ____   3 ____   4 ____   7 ____

Christopher Columbus 1 ____   6 ____   7 ____   8 ____

Michelle Kwan   2 ____   3 ____   5 ____   9 ____

Lance Armstrong   3 ____   4 ____   5 ____   9 ____

Kelly Clarkson   2 ____   3 ____   6 ____   9 ____

Derrek Lee   1 ____   2 ____   4 ____   8 ____

E. B. White   6 ____   7 ____   8 ____   9 ____

Carrie Underwood   2 ____   3 ____   5 ____   6 ____

Bill Clinton   1 ____   4 ____   7 ____   8 ____

Sasha Cohen   2 ____   3 ____   6 ____   9 ____

Amerigo Vespucci   5 ____   6 ____   7 ____   8 ____

HANGMAN

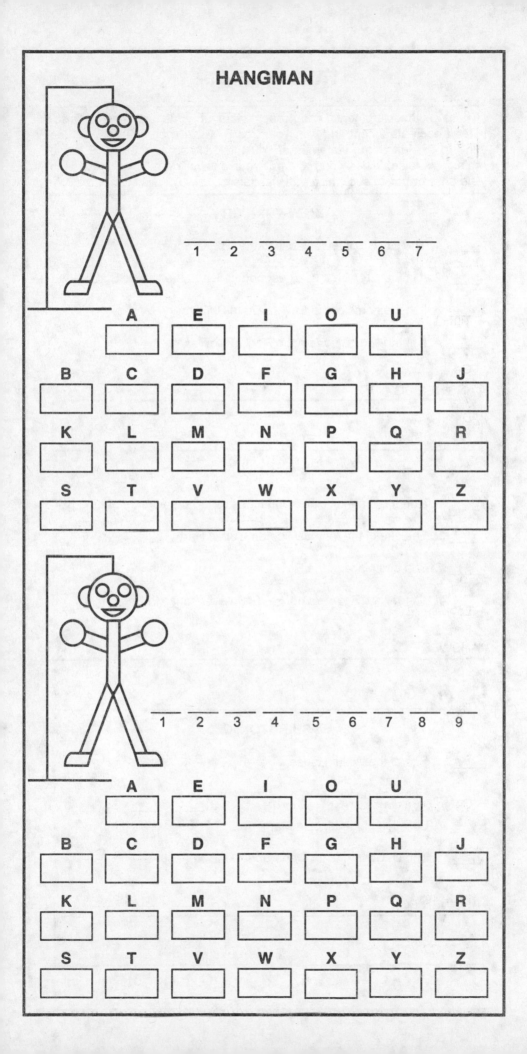

TRUE OR FALSE

Three of the statements about each state are true and one is false. Read each statement and with your Yes & Know® pen write a T on the line to the left of the statement if you think it is true; write an F if you think it is false. When you have put your answer on all four lines, fill in the answer box to see which one was false and why it was false.

NEW YORK CITY

_____ 1. The city is sometimes called the "Big Orange."

_____ 2. It is the city with the largest population in the United States.

_____ 3. It is the home of the Empire State Building.

_____ 4. It is the site of the famous Rockefeller Center.

ANSWER BOX:

BOSTON

_____ 1. Home of Faneuil Hall, sometimes called the "Cradle of Liberty."

_____ 2. The site of the famous Boston Coffee Party.

_____ 3. The birthplace of the Revolutionary War in America.

_____ 4. Site of Paul Revere's house, the oldest house in Boston.

ANSWER BOX:

WASHINGTON, D. C.

_____ 1. Site of the White House.

_____ 2. Home of the Washington Monument.

_____ 3. Location of the Lincoln Memorial.

_____ 4. The D. C. stands for Department of Congress.

ANSWER BOX:

TEST YOUR MEMORY

Study the picture carefully. Then turn to the next page to see how many questions you can answer correctly.

TEST YOUR MEMORY

How much do you remember about the picture? No fair looking back.

What is the picture about?
_____ a wicked giant   _____ Santa Claus
_____ Old King Cole   _____ the Easter Bunny

What is hanging on the wall?
_____ a picture of Mrs. Claus   _____ a clock
_____ a mirror   _____ a calendar

What does the sign outside say?
_____ Watch for Reindeer   _____ Workshop
_____ North Pole   _____ Parking for Sleighs Only

What did you see outside the window?
_____ a reindeer   _____ a penquin
_____ a polar bear   _____ an elf

What is Santa holding in his right hand?
_____ a pencil   _____ his gloves
_____ a glass of milk   _____ his glasses

What is Santa writing on his list?
_____ toys he needs to make   _____ names of good children
_____ the elves' work schedule _____ names of his reindeer

What date is circled on the calendar?
_____ 24   _____ 28
_____ 25   _____ 30

What is the elf who is sitting down doing?
_____ making a toy   _____ tying a bow
_____ bouncing a ball   _____ dressing a doll

How many elves are in the picture?
_____ two   _____ four
_____ three   _____ five

Who will get a new doll?
_____ Mary   _____ Carmel
_____ Susan   _____ Ellen

What stuffed animal is one of the elves holding?
_____ an elephant   _____ a tiger
_____ a giraffe   _____ a bear

Where is Santa's glove?
_____ on his hand   _____ on the floor
_____ under his belt   _____ in his pocket

BASKETBALL

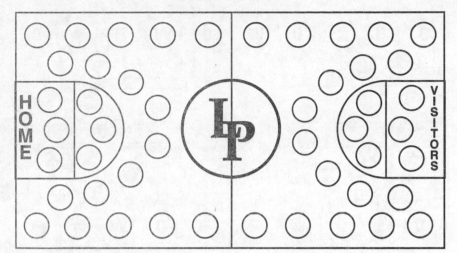

HOME

VISITORS

FREE THROW CHART

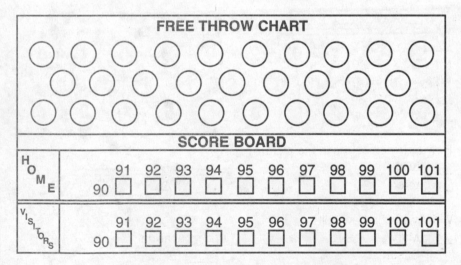

SCORE BOARD

HOME	90	91	92	93	94	95	96	97	98	99	100	101
		☐	☐	☐	☐	☐	☐	☐	☐	☐	☐	☐
VISITORS	90	91	92	93	94	95	96	97	98	99	100	101
		☐	☐	☐	☐	☐	☐	☐	☐	☐	☐	☐

LINE UP . . . CHOW TIME! . . . LINE UP

Flo Fisher, food fixer for the Farout Zoological Gardens, has just discovered a serious slip-up. Her $4,000 diamond ring somehow slipped off her finger and fell into one of the animal breakfast foods, but she doesn't know which one. She has to find it before breakfast time, which is only five minutes away.

See if you can put your finger on the correct food and help Flo find her ring before feeding time. Choose any clue to the right and fill in its answer space with your Yes & Know® pen. After each clue, try to find the ring by filling in the dotted area under the food you think the ring fell into. If NO appears, try another clue. If you find the food in one or two tries, Flo finds her ring and the animals get their food right on schedule. If it takes you three or four, Flo finds her ring, but only after some animal bent it out of shape. If it takes five or more, some animal has a very expensive breakfast.

CLUES

Has the ring fallen into a round package?

Does the weight appear on the package?

Does a star appear on the package?

Does an F appear on the package?

Does an even number appear on the package?

Has the ring fallen into a rectangular package?

Does an odd number appear on the package?

ANSWERS

FOOTBALL

TOUCHDOWN

START HERE

G   10   20   25   30   40   50   40   30   20   10   G

Down	RUNNING PLAYS						
1st							
2nd							
3rd							
4th							

Down	PASSING PLAYS				
1st					
2nd					
3rd					
4th					

TOUCHDOWN

START HERE

G   10   20   25   30   40   50   40   30   20   10   G

Down	RUNNING PLAYS						
1st							
2nd							
3rd							
4th							

Down	PASSING PLAYS				
1st					
2nd					
3rd					
4th					

WACKY WORLD OF WORDS

Complete the WACKYNITIONS below by choosing a word on the right. Use your Yes & Know® pen to write the letter of the word you choose on the line in front of the WACKYNITION™. Then go to the next page and see how many real definitions you can match with these same words.

_____ 1. A cabbage head has   A. Defense

_____ 2. Weatherman's forecast to his wife   B. Buccaneer

_____ 3. A group that sings in a church   C. Hanger-on

_____ 4. When Ashley pulled the puppy's tail he   D. Nobody

_____ 5. The room under the roof of a   E. Reindeer
        barn is called

_____ 6. When water is over your head, it is   F. Johnny-jump-up

_____ 7. The gate was locked so Clay climbed   G. Aloft

_____ 8. Emmy knows her puppy likes   H. Pasteurize
        her because

_____ 9. To hang the Mona Lisa, you need   I. Bitter
        a nail to

_____ 10. A tack in his seat made   J. Elixir

_____ 11. Price of fresh corn   K. Piggyback

_____ 12. Tom, Tom, the Piper's son should have   L. Acquire
        taken the

ANSWERS: Fill in the box to see how many you got right.

WONDERFUL WORLD OF WORDS

Complete the DEFINITIONS below by choosing a word on the right. Use your Yes & Know® pen to write the letter of the word you choose on the line in front of the DEFINITION.

_____ 1. Having a sharp, harsh, unpleasant taste   A. Defense

_____ 2. Far above the ground   B. Buccaneer

_____ 3. To gain or get as one's own   C. Hanger-on

_____ 4. Animal called caribou in North America   D. Nobody

_____ 5. On the back   E. Reindeer

_____ 6. Parasite   F. Johnny-jump-up

_____ 7. Guarding against attack   G. Aloft

_____ 8. No person   H. Pasteurize

_____ 9. Pirate   I. Bitter

_____ 10. A cure-all   J. Elixir

_____ 11. A popular name for the wild pansy; any one of various American violets   K. Piggyback

_____ 12. To heat liquids hot enough and long enough to kill harmful germs   L. Acquire

ANSWERS: Fill in the box to see how many you got right.